I0412132

ENFP: 33 Secrets From The Life of an ENFP

By Diana Jackson

Contents

ENFP: Extraverted, Intuitive, Feeing and Perceiving

1. Loves various social activities

Positive: ENFPs are the life of the party, and they love to keep busy. They have so much positive energy to spread, though, that they are never a nuisance and rarely into focusing all the attention on themselves, as some, more obnoxious people are wont to do. Instead, the ENFP is a welcome figure on any social scene, as they brighten and lighten the mood wherever they go.

Negative: ENFPs can get incredibly caught up in their social whirl, and may forget to take some time to themselves and just chill out. While they are capable of forward motion at a pretty frenetic and busy pace, they can overstep the limits of their energy and end up combusting before they ever stop to take a breath.

In Relationships: If you're dating an ENFP you better have a lot of different outfits and a lot of energy to keep up, because they'll take you wine tasting, horseback riding and then out to a club, all in one day (did you usually spend your Saturdays watching Netflix? Not anymore!). If anyone can get the ENFP to stop and just read a magazine quietly, though, it's their mate.

At Work: You might not entrust the ENFP to plan the office parties, but you know they'll show up with a mood-brightening attitude that gets everyone into the party spirit. Whether it's a party or a charity function or just showing up to represent at a 5K, the ENFP is the perfect face of your company wherever you need to put your best foot forward.

2. Passionate when inspired

Positive: ENFPs, as intuitive perceivers, are prone to coming up with a plethora of hugely inspired ideas that get them excited just thinking about them. When they can harness their energy and their focus long enough, the passion that bubbles up from within causes the ENFP to throw themselves into the project, using all of their formidable talents to will the idea into reality.

Negative: The downside is that ENFPs can find it incredibly difficult to actually focus. So while they might have an impossibly impassioned period when they are inspired to do or see something, without sensing or thinking functions, they can have a hard time actually figuring out how to go about rendering their idea into being. And when they get frustrated at the stalling of their amazing inspiration, they tend to just abandon ship and jump to something else.

In Relationships: For the partners of INFPs, there is nothing more inspiring than seeing their mate completely turned on and tuned into what they are doing, whether it's a personal website that they have loving crafted from top to bottom or a crusade to stop animal testing on dogs. Seeing someone act with passion is enough to incite romantic passion in a likewise fashion.

At Work: ENFPs are wonderful and popular people-persons, but their gifts are better suited to careers which give them independence and autonomy. So while their passion might not help the corporate world, charities, nonprofits, social services and service-based companies that need freelancers can all benefit from the enormous talents and energies of the engaged ENFP.

3. Inspires and motivates others

Positive: ENFPs don't often like to take leadership positions because the accompanying responsibility comes with a handful of obligations, but on a more individual level this personality type has the ability to inspire and motivate the people around them. And since ENFPs are thoughtful, caring, empathic people, they're usually inspiring people to follow their lead and do good.

Negative: Without a strong head for practicality or logical decision-making, however, ENFPs can go down a futile path and, unwittingly, take others with them. ENFPs are motivated to fight the good fight when necessary, and they are so charismatic that others are bound to follow, but when they only see one side of an issue, their judgment can be misplaced.

In Relationships: If the ENFP romantic partner doesn't inspire you to be a better version of yourself, no one will. Because of all their energy, ENFPs tend to be in good shape and enjoy physical activities, but they also love a good meal and can appreciate a sunset with the best of them. One of the ENFP's most enduring gifts to their mates is showing them how to recognize and love the small gifts in life.

At Work: As mentioned, you likely won't find the ENFP in a suit and a cubicle, but that just means that they can work out among the people who bustle around this world every day. And because they tend to have a touch of wanderlust, the ENFP usually takes their wild, wonderful and inspiring spirit global.

4. Good at talking their way into and out of situations

Positive: Need to get backstage at that Lady Gaga concert? Don't want the police officer to ticket you for speeding? Then keep your ENFP friend close, because these smooth-talking charmers could convince the birds to sing with them, Snow White-style. What's more, ENFPs naturally build up a strong network of friends in high places by virtue of their outgoing sociability, so they always know someone who owes them a favor.

Negative: Having a bit of a mouth is normally a good thing, but while ENFPs normally can brazen out any situation with just the right word, it's not always the case. And, without realizing it, they can get a little bit arrogant (or say, over-confident), truly offending the wrong person with their blatant attempt at a bribe or blackmail.

In Relationships: The ENFP's partner might not know quite what they are getting themselves into at first with this silver-tongued snake in the grass, but just a few weeks should make the situation clear enough. Hopefully they'll keep a sense of humor, even as they groan, "There she goes again..." as they stand back and watch their girlfriend talk her way into a celebrity after-party.

At Work: ENFPs, if they have enough freedom and independence in their career, can be wonderfully effective when they are deployed for coast-to-coast or international business deals. Sitting in the office isn't for them, but ad sales or something similar could be right up their alley, as close huge deals with company clients at the restaurants where they know the owners.

5. Can seem irresponsible

Positive: ENFPs actually take their missions in life seriously, but if they seem irresponsible, it's because they make a priority out of ordering their lives to allow the maximum amount of freedom. It might look effortless, but actually ENFPs put a lot of work into obtaining the lifestyles they want, so clearly the haters are underestimating them.

Negative: It is, however, part of the ENFP's make-up to have less regard for strict schedules and serious, "adult" responsibilities, and they themselves will be the first to admit that they struggle with practical, everyday tasks. People who view ENFPs as irresponsible are generally highlighting these types of characteristics and be blowing them out of proportion, but they do exist.

In Relationships: Everyone falls in love with the ENFP, and some might try to tame this wild spirit, but that can only end in catastrophe. Woe be unto the partner who, the more the ENFP displays irresponsible behavior, stiffens their resolve to bring this personality in line. It's a losing battle.

At Work: ENFPs only cement outsiders' impression of them as irresponsible by seeking out careers that might not seem like careers at all – party promoters, for instance, or freelance graphic designers. But make no mistake: ENFPs are busting their butts out there, the same as anyone else.

6. Kind, charming and amiable

Positive: ENFPs go out of their way to be the sort of person that they themselves would want to meet: a decent human being, kind and funny, easy to talk to and friendly. In so doing, they make the world a better place just by being themselves, because this aura of positive energy goes with them wherever they are heading (even the DMV, or the long line at Target on Christmas Eve).

Negative: Like other feeling types, the ENFP – who lacks a strong logical and reasoning center – can be vulnerable to manipulators and users. They put the best of themselves out there and rather naively assume that everyone else does the same, but there malicious people waiting in the wings, studying the situation and how they can take advantage of the ENFP.

In Relationships: ENFPs never have any trouble landing a date – their warm, kind personalities, combined with their obvious relish and love of life, is a natural magnet for any warm-blooded human within 100 miles. They can have difficulties holding onto one person for too long, though, as they are prone to flightiness and changes of opinion or emotion, and then they can have a tough time severing ties.

At Work: Put the ENFP out among the public with a mission to do good, and watch them shine. They love it so much that they'd probably do it for free, but luckily they can always put their people skills to good use and be able to pay the bills at the same time. With their innately kind and well-meaning natures, ENFPs make excellent counselors and therapists.

7. Can be disorganized and scatterbrained

Positive: If ENFPs can be disorganized and scatterbrained, it's usually not regarding something that is extremely important (they definitely have their priorities). In fact, for the rest of us, the ENFP's tendency toward brain-farts is one of their more endearing qualities, because this type is just so fun and cool – they seem too awesome and perfect to be real, but they definitely have less glowing qualities, like the rest of us.

Negative: Most rumors are rooted in fact, and most of the reputation that precedes the ENFP does have a small grain of truth. No, they're not going to forget their mother's birthday, but they might forget that they were supposed to meet a friend for lunch. They're lucky they have the ability to sweet-talk lions, because it's easy to get annoyed at the small details they forget (which add up over time).

In Relationships: It's probably best if ENFPs, both male and female, let their partner serve as the "head of household," in the sense that they are the ones to whom the responsibility of calling the plumber and paying the bills and doing the grocery shopping is delegated. ENFPs are just too busy thinking about their next great idea to consider the small matter of having electricity this month.

At Work: If there is one place that ENFPs feel as though they have a duty to others (a duty they don't resent), it's at work. ENFPs in the social services especially would never want their clients to feel as though they have been forgotten, so they will try extra hard to get their naturally disorganized mindset under control.

8. Great at parties and loves to have fun

Positive: If there really was one word to sum up the ENFP, it would be "fun." They just love to have a good time. Whereas a sensing type might think, "We should have gotten more tuna tartar for this party," intuitive ENFPs think big, calling in a favor and getting women in ball gowns to jump around in a the bouncy house that magically appeared in the parking lot of the hotel.

Negative: Life can seem like a party for the ENFP, who is nonetheless sensitive to others' criticism, especially when it's directed at their fun-loving lifestyle. To imply that they are lazy or are coasting through life by virtue of good looks or wealthy parents is one of the worst insults the ENFP can hear, and it's not even that bad. But, since ENFPs are used to everyone at parties loving them, even the smallest bit of criticism stings them hard.

In Relationships: If the ENFP finds a similarly sociable and outgoing partner, the two of them could rule the party scene no matter where they are (provided they have no jealousy or competitive issues). The ENFP might also benefit from dating someone a bit more sedate – someone who encourages them to take a break once in a while, skip a party, and stay home to read for one night.

At Work: ENFPs take the party with them wherever they go, so that even the bleakest job (if they should find themselves stuck in one) is at least a little bit more fun with this personality type around. Jobs that are based on a city's social scene, like party planning or club promoting, are right up the ENFP's alley.

9. Enjoys taking risks and living on the edge

Positive: We wouldn't have half the technology we have today if it weren't for risk-takers. And while ENFPs aren't born scientists, their ability to come up with edgy and futuristic ideas – that others with the technical skills can then transform into reality – marks them out as pioneers in the world today.

Negative: Some of the risks ENFPs are willing to take can involve a startling amount of physicality, like sky-driving; they can also find themselves up to their eyeballs in debt, because they got addicted to high-stakes gambling. They might even end up with a bloody nose because they took a risk and said something they shouldn't have to the wrong person.

In Relationships: Any personality type can cheat, but the thrill of deception in relationships is going to be vastly appealing to the ENFP, particularly because their perceiving aspect influences the frequency with which they skip around in their desires. In order to show the kindness that they are renowned for, ENFPs have to learn to cut ties rather than cheat.

At Work: ENFPs can be excellent in marketing and advertising, because they not only have their fingers on the pulse of what people want and how to best appeal to them, but they are willing to try the edgier ad campaign that is going to get a lot of people talking. Sure, there might be some misses in terms of judgment, but it's like the saying goes: "All press is good press."

10. Much more sensitive than insensitive

Positive: ENFPs have big personalities, but unlike thinking types, they are also firmly committed to using all the energy they have to help others. Plus, they are themselves personally sensitive, and so, knowing how it makes them feel when they are criticized keeps them from saying the rude or critical thing almost every time.

Negative: ENFPs can end up showing sensitivity and kindness to people who have proven they don't deserve it, and then live to regret it (like the good guy who pulls the bad guy up off the ledge they were dangling from, only to get shot). ENFPs are also sensitive in the sense that they have a difficult time hearing negative things about themselves from others.

In Relationships: Despite the fact that ENFPs love a big crowd, when they are one-on-one with their sweeties they could not be more thoughtful or considerate of that person's feelings. In fact, even when they are among a big group of friends and acquaintances, the ENFP is still thinking of their loved one – it's the only thing that could make them want to head home early.

At Work: As sensitive souls, ENFPs have a deft touch when it comes to handling people, so they make good negotiators and even diplomats, if they can harness their unpredictability and take on a more buttoned-up career. But they are equally sensitive to criticism for the work they do, so they have to grow thicker skin.

11. Readily affectionate

Positive: ENFPs do more than just touch people's lives with their ready kindness and generosity; they are willing to literally reach out, with their own two arms, and give a hug where a hug is clearly needed. Affectionate and warm, ENFPs don't care if you are getting over a cold if you need a literal shoulder to cry on.

Negative: ENFPs might not think anything of reaching out and touching a stranger on the shoulder during a conversation, but others aren't quite so demonstrative, and it can make them shrink away from the situation. ENFPs have to make sure they are reading a person's body language properly before making physical touch-contact with someone they don't know well.

In Relationships: If there is one person with whom the ENFP happily makes contact at every possible moment, it is their partner, so cold fishes need not apply. ENFPs partners can feel the literal warmth of their mates every day, a reassuring envelop of love and affection in the form of hugs, kisses and more intimate acts.

At Work: ENFPs have an especial affinity for children, who still have the creative wonder that erodes away in most other types of adults. ENFPs are exceptionally good nannies and caretakers for kids, would do well in daycares or as child counselors. They are ready with the hugs when children need them most and will happily let a child play on their lap at blocks or a puzzle.

12. Energized by being around other people

Positive: It really is an advantage when people like the ENFP are energized by the company of others, because humans are social creatures and our world is one in which people are meant to interact face-to-face. Just by going to the mall, the ENFP can pick up the excitement and the hope that shoppers exhibit, and then they can take that with them wherever else they go.

Negative: If the ENFP falls ill for a week, and they cannot go out and be among groups of people and socialize, their energy can get incredibly sapped and it can be difficult for them to exhibit the exuberant creativity and independence that marks their personality. ENFPs have to learn how to keep their stores of passion engaged, even if they aren't out and about, mixing with company.

In Relationships: Having just one other person around can make the ENFP more likely to stick around at home for a night (though they might be thinking about the new restaurant opening that they are missing). Still, being able to interact with someone they care about on a romantic level is very exciting for ENFPs.

At Work: INFPs and ENFPs could do a lot of the same jobs, but the difference is that careers which are very social require the INFP to withdraw at some point and to re-energize, while the ENFP is like a cell phone that is always plugged in and at 100 percent battery power.

13. Can be unprepared

Positive: While ENFPs do have a tendency to under-prepare for the situations they find themselves in, both personal and professional, they come fully equipped with the charisma to brazen them out. So they showed up at a black-tie gala in jeans? No biggie, they'll turn it into a brilliantly witty joke that precedes them wherever they go.

Negative: If the ENFP gets caught in a snow storm and ends up stranded on the side of the road, you can bet their cell phone is down to five percent battery and they have no snow brush in their car. ENFPs: making bad situations worse for themselves since the dawn of time.

In Relationships: Actually, the thing ENFPs are most unprepared for in their personal lives is how hard relationships and marriage really are. With movies and TV making love look like an easy walk in the park, ENFPs can come ill-equipped to adult relationships, with an idealized notion of how things are supposed to work.

At Work: One of the worst places to be unprepared is the work environment, but ENFPs are fairly good at seeking out careers which allow for their less organized trait to fly under the radar. By steering clear of management or leadership positions or even becoming self-employed, ENFPs can mitigate the damage of an unprepared lifestyle.

14. Loves to try new things

Positive: New food? New bar? New electric car? Yes, please, the ENFP says, sign me up! Their exuberance in life is at least partially a side-effect of their willingness to go where they never have gone before, always keeping an open mind and never writing off anything until they have actually tried it.

Negative: Sometimes – rarely, not often, but still on occasion – trying something new can end disastrously. Like the time the ENFP went for the sashimi for the first time and learned they have an allergy. Or when they had to try skydiving and their parachute gave them about 10 seconds of heart failure before deploying. ENFPs would also benefit from finding one or two things they love and sticking with them.

In Relationships: ENFPs like to try new things with their partners as a way of getting to know each other better. But they equally like to try new relationships, to see what makes someone else fun and exciting. With that said, it can take the ENFP longer than average to settle down (they're just having too much fun to get married and start a family!).

At Work: Whereas more uptight, traditionally-minded employees would be less likely to try a new technique or technology, ENFPs gladly welcome the opportunity with an open mind and open arms. For ENFPs, you never know if a method is going to be the new best way to do something unless you actually try.

15. Broadly talented and skilled

Positive: A lot of ENFPs are triple-threats or more – they have the skills to do many different things better than your average Joe. This means that when they aren't working, they are likely engaging in some hobby, whether it's quiet painting in the park or skiing down the highest mountain in their region.

Negative: Because ENFPs find that they are good at so many things, it can be difficult for them to find focus and stability in their lives. The ENFPs who is good at both painting and skiing might pursue both hobbies, traveling far and wide and never putting down real roots or forging a real home to come back to.

In Relationships: ENFPs are more than likely to meet potential mates while they are out doing something they love (and looking so attractive in the process). They're going to be the coolest-looking people who ever went paintballing or the hottest beach bod on the sand during a volleyball game with friends – and no one will be able to take their eyes off of them.

At Work: Another area where ENFPs can run into trouble making a choice in their life is where their job is concerned. Everything is appealing to the ENFP, and they in turn are appealing to most employers (on the surface, at least). ENFPs have to think long and hard about what they really want to do.

16. Project-oriented

Positive: Tell your ENFP buddy that you need help "on a project" and they are there, no questions asked, ready and enthusiastic. On their own time, ENFPs like to pursue life as a series of larger goals – going to Fiji by the end of the year or getting a dog and being the best pet owner ever – that sound fun, exciting and adventurous.

Negative: ENFPs don't really seem to know what to do with downtime. Even when they do finally stop moving and just hang out on the couch with a bowl of cereal and Netflix, they are thinking about where they want to go and what they want to do as soon as they change out of these sweatpants. Yet they are just as capable of burning out (or burning through all their money) as anyone else.

In Relationships: The partners of ENFPs often find themselves accompanying their mates on whatever project has captured their fancy this week, and for someone with an open mind and an open heart, this suits them just fine. A flexible mate who doesn't mind letting someone else take the lead (and lead them on into trouble) would be a good match for the spontaneous ENFP.

At Work: In the workplace, ENFPs are at their best when they have a project about which they feel passionately. All the negative parts of their personality – the lack of organization, the tendency to be unprepared – fall away, because an ENFP on a mission is focused and determined.

17. Thoroughly adventurous

Positive: ENFPs goes to great lengths to keep their lifestyle flexible, so that if a camping trip in Europe comes up, they can leave at a moment's notice. But it's not just international travel that appeals to the ENFP's senses; they're the first to jump off a high bridge into the river below, the one who wants to take up trapeze artistry. The life of an ENFP is never boring.

Negative: Pose a challenge to the ENFP, throw down the gauntlet, and they can't resist. But sometimes, they really should. ENFPs would much rather spend their time gallivanting and having fun, but their credit cards can end up maxed out as they have no other way to pay for such an extravagantly lived lifestyle.

In Relationships: If you stick around with your ENFP mate long enough, you will be able to watch in wonder as they proclaim their desire to head out on a great adventure and then will it into being. If you're lucky and brave enough, you'll accompany them and experience things that you'll remember forever.

At Work: ENFPs are terrific when it comes to international travel, so they might do well as flight attendants (they certainly have the people skills!) or professional adventurers who work for clients in various capacities to seek out objects or people all around the world. No task is too dangerous; the ENFP is confident they can get themselves in and out of any situation, after all.

18. Changes careers more often than usual

Positive: A lot of people spend years and years in a career that they hate, figuring what's the point in leaving? They'll just have to start over again somewhere else. ENFPs are particularly sensitive about what they do for a living, refusing to be tied down to a career that they aren't excited about every morning, ensuring that their passionate enthusiasm is life-long.

Negative: The problem with changing careers a whole lot of times throughout your life is just that: there's no stability or putting down of roots. ENFPs are particularly happy flitting through life like a butterfly in a garden full of beautiful flowers, but at some point that lifestyle can become empty and meaningless. And ENFPs won't know where to start when they want to live more meaningfully.

In Relationships: It can be incredibly frustrating for the ENFP's partner to watch their mate go from job to job, switching between beauty school and nail artistry to yoga instructor to Flamenco dancer. More tolerant and likewise open-minded personalities can be supportive for years, but the traditional mates will balk in no time at the career-jumping.

At Work: Frankly, ENFPs are fine moving around from job to job, because they like new experiences and tapping into hitherto uncovered talents and passions. With their indomitable courage and easy charm, they can make themselves welcome in any field and any crowd.

19. Very spontaneous

Positive: Random girls' weekend in Vegas? Check. Career change overnight? On it. Brand new set of wheels because he's had the old ones for a year? You know it. ENFPs male and female both live their lives as a tribute to the moment, happily pursuing whatever path looks like it's the most fun. These types always have a great story to tell about the last random, crazy thing they did.

Negative: Spontaneity now and then is not a bad thing at all, but ENFPs have a way of pushing situations to the limits of reason and beyond, oftentimes making bad choices that seemed great at the time, but because they didn't think them through, end up causing more harm than happiness. ENFPs have a particular talent for maxing out credit cards, too.

In Relationships: ENFPs are happiest when partnered up with a mate who can keep up – or better yet, apace – with their joyful need for speed and stimulation. One of the issues this personality type runs into is that they meet someone who starts out as spontaneous as them, but the other person eventually runs out of steam – and the ENFP starts to view that person as a real drag.

At Work: ENFPs are the types of people who thrive in careers where they are required to travel, even if it's at the drop of a hat. In fact, they love waking up every morning not knowing where they'll end the day, and because they are less likely to put down roots until much later in their lives (if ever), traveling is a real pleasure, not a burden while they are younger.

20. Finds meaning and value in everything/everyone

Positive: True intuitives, ENFPs are more likely to believe in the idea of fate, and will go to great lengths in their rare downtime (say, when they're on an international flight) to connect the dots between their experiences and acquaintances. This might not be everyone's style, but for the ENFP it brings them a great deal of comfort and, for a type that doesn't settle, a kind of stability.

Negative: Sometimes situations and people just are, with no rhyme or reason, but the ENFP can drive themselves crazy trying to figure out what an action or a statement meant, or what the latest "sign" to appear in their life is trying to tell them. Too often, ENFPs will take the easy route and decide it all means what they want it to mean, despite more discerning heads telling them otherwise.

In Relationships: ENFPs have a tendency to go through a lot of relationships (and there's nothing wrong with that!). While they might end up heartbroken after the end of every relationship, ENFPs are plucky in the sense that they look at it as an experience from which they learned or gained new insight, and they certainly feel as though that person was placed in their life for a reason.

At Work: ENFPs are social creatures by nature who love to interact with others, but their love of conversation is deeper than what it seems on the surface. They are deeply caring and compassionate people who like to find out what makes others tick, and for this reason ENFPs are excellent counselors, therapists and even life coaches, because they believe that everyone has a purpose in life.

21. Always seeking inner peace

Positive: Despite how carefree and wild they might live, ENFPs are sensitive souls who place "inner peace and happiness" high on their list of priorities. How they go about finding that peace might be different from everyone else out there, but their pursuit is genuine and sincere. In fact, perhaps if more people tried to be happy with and proud of who they are – if more people learned to like themselves – the world would be a better place.

Negative: As mentioned, ENFPs come to a place of personal understanding and acceptance differently than others. For them, it could be hiking in the wilderness of the Sedona desert for two days, totally off the grid, without any way of contacting them. While this might bring the ENPF a great deal of spiritual and emotional enlightenment, their families could be frantic to locate them in the meantime.

In Relationships: ENFPs might have a difficult time truly coming to a place of total accord with themselves because they may find themselves trying to fit someone else into their lives who doesn't mesh – and they can make this same effort over and over, many times over the course of their lives, blaming themselves for the fact that it isn't working, when it's really a matter of mutual compatibility.

At Work: One of the reasons ENFPs jump from job to job is because they are seeking that occupation that is fulfilling on every level – in essence, that "perfect" job, which likely doesn't exist; no job is perfect. ENFPs might have this ideal in mind, which can never be obtained, and so their search goes on, again and again. If they're very lucky, though, they will find something deeply soul-satisfying.

22. Intense about their values

Positive: While it is usually the sensing types who hold to their values very tightly, ENFPs are just as intense because their values are what informs their lifestyle, which they work very hard to maintain. For a personality that can be viewed from the outside as flighty or superficial by detractors, this gives ENFPs a much-needed dose of seriousness.

Negative: When the ENFP's values come under fire, however, rather than react mildly to the persecution, shaking it off like nothing, this personality type – who is constantly pulsing with energy – can go straight to attack mode. If her ancient aunt suggests that she should "consider settling down," the fiercely independent ENFP can shoot back with a stinging response that blows the comment out of proportion.

In Relationships: Simply put, if their potential partner doesn't agree with their values and the way the ENFP chooses to live his or her life, he or she has no use for them. They're not going to stick around with someone who will try to change them, which is really to their credit. Feeling types tend to consider others' emotions in their decision-making, but the ENFP lifestyle is one place where they don't budge.

At Work: Another reason ENFPs can jump from job to job is because what starts out as a "perfect" gig can turn into a real drag – for instance, they won't let the ENFP take a week off once a month to visit friends all over the world. Because spontaneity is such an integral part of who the ENFP is, they'd rather quit than compromise their happiness.

23. Scattered, easily changes focus

Positive: ENFPs aren't ones to dwell on anything for too long, so if something bad happens in their life, they are quick to move on. That's not to say they don't feel the hurt, because they are sensitive and kind and appreciate the same from others; but if something is distasteful for them, they can easily find something else to focus on instead.

Negative: ENFPs are floaters who happily go wherever the wind blows them, and while it's not for anyone else to judge them when they are content, they themselves can reach a point in their lives where they have something like an existential crisis. While they have a specific point of view, a lot of ENFPs can't focus long enough for it to come to fruition in any meaningful way.

In Relationships: ENFPs don't just forget birthday or anniversaries sometimes – they can lose their focus when it comes to the person they are with, especially if someone new comes along who seems to fulfill everything that their current partner is lacking. For a certainty, ENFPs don't mean to hurt anyone, but it can happen on a regular basis.

At Work: On the one hand, ENFPs are quite valuable in a fast-paced workplace where the focus shifts can leave others in the dust; but on the other, ENFPs need to be able to harness their energy in one direction for long enough to actually see projects through from start to finish.

24. Dislikes rules

Positive: There are absolutely some areas in life where the rules need to be chucked and the traditions should be overturned. ENFPs aren't the most logical or well-reasoned personalities, but they have a strong sense of social justice and equality, so even if company policy proclaims the customer is always right, this type is going to stand up for the cashier getting yelled at by an irrationally angry idiot.

Negative: The ENFP isn't terribly discerning when it comes to disliking rules – they don't favor most of them and feel the rules don't apply them. This includes some laws. So the ENFP is, unfortunately, more likely to view petty theft, like shoplifting a candy bar, to be a funny foible, not a crime. But that's just the thing: it *is* a crime, and they *are* hurting people by doing it.

In Relationships: ENFPs are more likely to conduct nontraditional relationships, whether it's dating for decades and never getting married or even dabbling in lifestyles like polyamory. What's certain is that while their relatives might wonder every year, when is that ENFP going to settle down and have kids, they themselves are more concerned about living in the now and having as much fun as possible.

At Work: ENFPs almost have to take on nontraditional careers, because jobs where there are a lot of rules and restrictions are going to have them chafing at the bit to be free. Even in more independent or liberal careers, ENFPs are going to bend the rules whenever they can, and the outcome is anyone's guess.

25. Values interpersonal relationships

Positive: ENFPs don't just talk to people to fill time or space; they genuinely care about the well-being of others, and in a way they consider it their duty or mission to unearth the hidden meanings in human behavior and thought. For a type that is often pegged as unfocused or without perspective, ENFPs have a very committed, if subtle, goal in life, and even if it doesn't help people continents away, it does help the people the ENFP comes into contact with.

Negative: Caring about relationships with people and having a high emotional intelligence are wonderful traits, but the balance is tipped so far in that direction that ENFPs are generally sorely lacking in practical skills and logical thinking habits. They'll know what to say to someone who is injured in a car accident but not how to provide the rudimentary medical care that could save their life before paramedics arrive.

In Relationships: ENFPs tend to make devoted slaves out of their romantic partners (which can certainly be tricky during the extraction phase), not because they are domineering or controlling, but because they are so good at understanding people. And when someone feel as though another person truly "gets" them, they want to cling to that person forever.

At Work: Even if ENFPs don't work in the social services or counseling fields, their ability to "read" people is a very handy skill that can, when they find the focus, lead them to extraordinary professional success in fields where you might not expect to find them, like business (though you can expect them to err on the side of entrepreneur, rather than corporate suit).

26. Wants to be accepted

Positive: There are some personality types who couldn't care less what others think about them, and while that's admirable, it can give them an excuse to treat people badly. ENFPs, on the other hand, want to be liked. They're already kind and generous as part of their nature, but they make sure to extend these traits to everyone they meet, making the world a much pleasanter place to be.

Negative: People who strive to be accepted have a tendency to do things they wouldn't normally do or compromise who they are. They can also be manipulated by people for whom they are changing in order to fit in. ENFPs are always in danger of falling victim to either of these situations and not realizing it until it's too late.

In Relationships: At the beginning a relationship, the ENFP wants very much for their new partner to find them irresistible. They don't have to try too hard – ENFPs are, by nature, quite desirable – but this desire to be accepted and loved by their mate is one of traits which make them even more endearing.

At Work: Wherever the ENFP goes professionally, he or she is deeply flattering and ingratiating, as a way of fostering good relationships between coworkers and authorities, as well as any clients they might handle. It's not at all insincere, and in fact, it's what makes ENFPs such good ambassadors for whoever has them in their employ.

27. Prone to hyperactivity

Positive: Unlike kids with too much sugar in them, ENFPs can actually sit still, provided they're sitting still and doing something, like painting or having a nice meal. So their hyperactivity has to do with their needing to be constantly doing something, and it enriches their lives to have many experiences under their belts.

Negative: The ENFP's hyperactivity might suit them well, but it can be exhausting for their friends and family, who never know where they'll show up or when. It's not that ENFPs are children who should have to check in with anyone, but they can get so wrapped up in their latest vision quest that they don't touch base for months, worrying plenty of people.

In Relationships: Hopefully the partners of ENFPs aren't couch potatoes, because they're going to get their butts kicked trying to keep up with their hyperactive partners. These personality types vibe best with people who have similar energy levels; what could be better than traveling through life at a sprint, with someone right next to you?

At Work: If you can't beat 'em, join 'em – or rather, if you can't keep the ENFP in one place, then give him or her a position where they can take advantage of their hyperactive preferences. A lot of people dread positions where they have to travel and be away from their families, but getting to jump on a plane once a week and head somewhere new sounds like heaven to the ENFP.

28. Adept at understanding other people's POVs

Positive: With their empathic and sensitive natures, as well as their propensity for traveling far and wide, all the while absorbing the nuances and subtleties of culture and language, ENFPs are born diplomats and activists, whether it's a matter abroad, like access to clean drinking water, or something closer to home, like the effects of poverty on inner-city children.

Negative: ENFPs are sponges, soaking up their own experiences, but also the experiences of others as relayed to them, and while they are very good at lending a sympathetic ear or taking a stand against injustice, they are also rather disorganized and unfocused; so despite meaning to do good with the knowledge they have from others' POVs, oftentimes their efforts stop at words.

In Relationships: ENFPs might not always do what they know you want them to do, but at least they understand why you want them to do it. In relationships, ENFPs tend to reach a point with more traditional partners where they recognize that person wants them to settle down; they understand why it's important to them, but at the same time, they aren't going to do it and put an end to their lifestyle.

At Work: ENFPs are very sympathetic, but they are also something like a secret weapon that can be deployed in situations where the other parties' intent or need must be found out. ENFPs are like emotional spies, able to charm others and ingratiate themselves into confidences, gleaning the information they need to subtly manipulate.

29. Not concerned with the details of everyday life

Positive: ENFPs are fairly certain that they know the secret to enjoying life: not taking anything too seriously, including themselves and the boring life details that slow you down or hold you back. This might not vibe with everyone (indeed, the majority of people out there would be uncomfortable living with this POV), but the ENFP has a way of making it work.

Negative: It is fortunate that ENFPs have a way with people, because they'll need to be able to charm their landlord into letting that seventh late payment slide. It's a shame that ENFPs don't concern themselves with the details of everyday life, especially the ones that make having a permanent home possible, because they are capable of creating an innovative oasis in a sea of boring houses.

In Relationships: Sometimes the ENFP will find that mate who embodies the idea of "opposites attract." Sometimes there exists a love powerful enough to overcome the differences that ENFPs have with a lot of people out there, and they find themselves balanced by a more detail-oriented mate, who in turn learns to relish and enjoy life and spontaneity.

At Work: ENFPs are not the people to turn to for practical advice about making life more organized. However, they are precisely the people you want to talk to if you need to make sense of your experiences thus far and figure out how you have come to be in your present predicament. Laugh if you want, but ENFPs would make terrific psychics.

30. Impulsive

Positive: For the ENFP, life is all about possibility. These personality types can seem as though they have lived three or four lifetimes by the time they hit 40, and this is because they never back down from a challenge and they learn to just say "yes" without overthinking. Impulsiveness is the opposite of boring, and so are ENFPs.

Negative: ENFPs like to live on the edge, but there are consequences to that. They can find themselves in severe financial straits because they would rather have fun than work, and they can find that the people about whom they care the most are alienated by the differences in lifestyle and perspective. These types shouldn't have to change who they are to fit someone else's standards, but tempering their impulsiveness would be advised.

In Relationships: There are lots of ways impulsivity can affect the ENFP in relationships. This can range from opening the door to a new one (by randomly kissing a stranger) to ending an old one (by being unfaithful when they truly did not mean to be). ENFPs are never dull company, but they can be heartbreakers.

At Work: Without impulsive people pushing the limits and taking chances, our society would be nowhere near as advanced. ENFPs make up part of that group of innovators and world-shakers who are willing to try something professionally just for the sake of novelty and the possibility that it could be great.

31. Has a need to explore

Positive: Curiosity might have killed the cat, but it makes the ENFP a well-traveled, emotionally sensitive and intelligent diplomat. There are few personality types that are so willing to forgo roots and embrace the unknown – which could explain why their names end up becoming so famous, like Mark Twain and Bill Clinton.

Negative: Without coming across like a spy show on TV, ENFPs actually run a high risk of becoming embroiled in situations that they shouldn't be, simply because they couldn't leave well enough alone. Political scandals, international military crises – there's probably an ENFP stuck in the middle of it somehow.

In Relationships: ENFPs don't just want to explore cliffs and caves and restaurants and cities with their significant others; they're also interesting in exploring the limits and boundaries of relationship itself, and may suggest nontraditional lifestyles and activities. Squeamish or close-minded personalities need not apply!

At Work: ENFPs are happiest in the workplace if they have room to explore ideas and concepts, most of which are people-centric. Let the ENFP try a new form of therapy to help people suffering from PTSD or give them free reign to implement a new, more intuitive schedule at a daycare. And try not to criticize the ENFP for wanting to explore new career options regularly.

32. Actively avoids strict schedules and obligations

Positive: If you have a random weekend free and you'd like your ENFP friend to join you, chances are good that he or she is on board. In more dire situations, if you need a helping hand after popping a tire on the highway, the ENFP isn't stuck behind a desk and unable help you, no – they can hop in their car and come to your rescue.

Negative: Taking on stricter schedules and obligations is a sign of growing up, maturing. We live the first 20 or so years of our lives in relatively irresponsibility, but at that point, many of us begin to grow up. ENFPs can seem like they are stunted developmentally because they refuse to take on the responsibilities that everyone else shoulders.

In Relationships: The only thing ENFPs are willing to put in their datebooks in pen are vacations, and even those could change if something else comes up. It can be maddening for ENFPs' partners to try to make plans with their mates, but they either have to learn to roll with it or move on – these personality types aren't going to change.

At Work: ENFPs prefer a social career, but they were born to freelance, so if they work in fields where they interface with clients often, they'll be happiest and most fulfilled. ENFPs are usually gifted writers or artists, but they can also freelance as consultants, and business-minded ENFPs can try their hand at something like HR consulting.

33. Desires independence above all

Positive: ENFPs might crave the acceptance and love of others, but they are physically and intellectually independent. While their lifestyle might have all the planning of a wild frat party, ENFPs take great pains to do what needs to be done so that they are self-sustaining.

Negative: The ENFP's desire for independence, no matter what the cost, can indeed cost them quite a bit, from home and financial stability to friends and family members. Not everyone can just go along with the ENFP, and there is plenty of room for disagreement and argument, disillusionment and emptiness.

In Relationships: ENFPs are generally happy to be "independently together" – meaning that they are with someone, but have the space and freedom to live their life the way they always have. If their significant other chooses to tag along, they are more than welcome, but the second they try to lasso the ENFP, they'll get kicked to the curb.

At Work: ENFPs don't want anyone telling them what to do or how to do it, so clearly this personality type is not cut out for corporate work. Instead, independent enterprises like owning a small business or freelance endeavors are their best bet, since they can make their own schedule and don't have to answer to anyone except themselves.

www.ingramcontent.com/pod-product-compliance
Lightning Source LLC
Chambersburg PA
CBHW070503290526

45790CB00003B/1079